W9-CEA-718

# The Many Lives of Pusheen the Cat

## Also by Claire Belton

*I Am Pusheen the Cat*

*Pusheen Coloring Book*

*Mini Pusheen Coloring Book*

*Let's Bake!: A Pusheen Cookbook*

# The Many Lives of Pusheen the Cat

Claire Belton

Gallery Books
New York London Toronto Sydney New Delhi

Gallery Books
An Imprint of Simon & Schuster, Inc.
1230 Avenue of the Americas
New York, NY 10020

Copyright © 2021 by Pusheen Corp.

All rights reserved, including the right to reproduce this book or portions thereof in any form whatsoever. For information, address Gallery Books Subsidiary Rights Department, 1230 Avenue of the Americas, New York, NY 10020.

First Gallery Books trade paperback edition March 2021

GALLERY BOOKS and colophon are registered trademarks of Simon & Schuster, Inc.

For information about special discounts for bulk purchases, please contact Simon & Schuster Special Sales at 1-866-506-1949 or business@simonandschuster.com.

The Simon & Schuster Speakers Bureau can bring authors to your live event. For more information or to book an event, contact the Simon & Schuster Speakers Bureau at 1-866-248-3049 or visit our website at www.simonspeakers.com.

Interior design by Jaime Putorti

Manufactured in the United States of America

1 3 5 7 9 10 8 6 4 2

Library of Congress Cataloging-in-Publication Data

Names: Belton, Claire, author.
Title: The many lives of Pusheen the cat / Claire Belton.
Description: First Gallery Books trade paperback edition. | New York : Gallery Books, 2021.
Identifiers: LCCN 2020049516 (print) | LCCN 2020049517 (ebook) | ISBN 9781982165390 (paperback) | ISBN 9781982165406 (ebook)
Subjects: LCSH: Cats—Humor. | Cats—Caricatures and cartoons. | Wit and humor, Pictorial.
Classification: LCC PN6231.C23 B45 2013 (print) | LCC PN6231.C23 (ebook) | DDC 741.5/6—dc23
LC record available at https://lccn.loc.gov/2020049516
LC ebook record available at https://lccn.loc.gov/2020049517

ISBN 978-1-9821-6539-0
ISBN 978-1-9821-6540-6 (ebook)

*For Sarah and Jake*

# Contents

Pusheen • 1

Pusheenicorn • 69

Super Pusheenicorn • 85

Mermaid Pusheen • 93

Pusheenosaurus & Dinosheens • 111

Pastel Pusheens • 125

Dragonsheen • 143

Detective Pusheen • 161

Pugsheen • 169

Acknowledgments • 179

# Pusheen

**GENDER:** Girl

**BIRTHDAY:** February 18

**BEST FEATURE:** Toes that look like beans

**FAVORITE FOOD:** All of them

**FAVORITE COLOR:** Cream

**HOBBIES:** Snacking, sleeping, blogging

**ATTRIBUTES:** Sweet, curious, lazy

# Types of Cat Tails

The noodle

The duster

The pine tree

The bottle brush

The question mark

The warning

# Events Suitable for Cats

Live music

Parades

Theater

Fine dining

# Tips for Sleeping Well

Cozy up your area

Get relaxed

Have a nice bath

Keep a routine

# Patterns That Cats Like

Tiger print

Leopard print

Snow leopard print

Cheetah print

Ikat

~~Houndstooth~~

YOU WANNA
PIZZA ME?

# A Study of Toe Beans

Beans

Bean sprouts

Broad beans

String beans

# Adulting Essentials

Meal planning

Commuting

Making dough

Getting bread

# How to Be a Good Roommate

Help with the laundry

Keep things tidy

Keep a low profile

Respect their privacy

# Catfé Drinks

Iced catpusheeno

Meowchiato

Affocato

Espurresso

# How to Make Purrfect Coffee

Gather your tools

Use quality beans

Pour nice and slow

Serve with snacks

# Where to Find Your Cat

1. Under the table

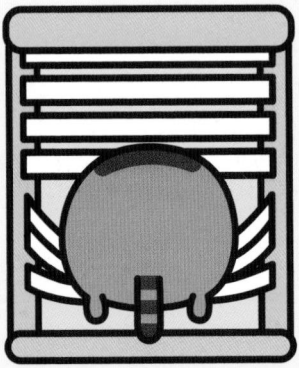

2. Behind the blinds

3. Inside the (empty) tub

4. In your business

# Reasons I Love Summer

Camping

Fairs

Water parks

Air-conditioning

# Nicknames for Your Cat

Bun

Roll

Loaf

Food made of flour, water, and yeast or another leavening agent mixed together and baked

# How to Have a *Perfect Birthday*

Wake up

Eat up

Level up

~~Grow up~~

# Pusheen's Guide to *Relaxing*

Wear a fuzzy robe

Have a hot drink

Put on comfy slippers

So. Relaxed.

# The Scents of Fall

Crunchy leaves

Cozy fires

Ripe apples

Despair

~~Early snow~~

# Halloween Activities
## for Your Cat

Dress up spooky

Do some tricks

Eat some treats

Play with wrappers

# Pusheen's Guide to Cakes

Cupcake

Birthday cake

Pancake

Patty-cake

# Traveling

## with Pusheen the Cat

Expectation

Reality

Expectation

Reality

Expectation

Reality

I kinda
like you

# Pusheen's Guide to *Household Chores*

Do the laundry

Wash the dishes

**Dust the shelves**

~~Vacuum~~

# How to Play Baseball

Make the most of left field

Catch what's important

Load the bases

Steal home

# Pusheen's Guide to a Balanced Diet

1. Sweet snacks

2. Salty snacks

3. Sweet snacks

4. Salty snacks

# Today's Menu

Breakfast:
waffles

Lunch:
sandwiches

Dinner:
frozen food

# 6 Reasons to Be Thankful for Your Cat

Warms your heart

Warms your seat

Cuddle buddy

Alarm clock buddy

Beautiful friend

Beautiful paperweight

# How to Make a Muffin

1. You will need a bowl

2. Get in that bowl

3. Nice work

# Pool Party Essentials

Shades

Shades

Wings

Wings

A float

A float

# Places I Sat Yesterday

7 a.m.: a chair

12 p.m.: a floor

5 p.m.: a desk

10 p.m.: a bed

# Learning to Speak Cat:
## Essential Phrases

Nah

Nuh-uh

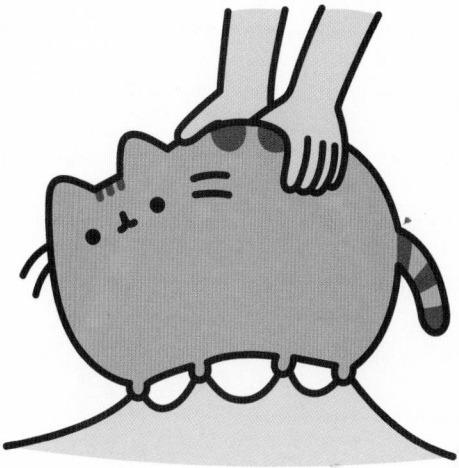

Nope

Absolutely not

# Dinner: A How-To

Yell

Shout

Whine

Dine!

# Gaming for Cats

Expectation

Reality

Expectation

Reality

Expectation

Reality

# Pusheen's Guide to Houseplants

Water regularly

But not too much

Provide lots of sun

But not too bright

Faux is fine

# Proper Dining Etiquette (for Your Cat)

Greet your server

Order your meal

Receive your meal

Send it back

# Complex Cat Emotions

**Hangry**
(hungry + angry)

**Borky**
(bored + frisky)

**Pleepy**
**(pleased + sleepy)**

**Fundignified**
**(fun + undignified)**

# Social Media for Cats

Twitter

TikTok

Facebook

Instagram

# Where to Find a Snack

In a drawer

In a jar

In a bag

In a mirror

# Physics with Your Cat

Magnetic energy

Thermal energy

Kinetic energy

# Pusheenicorn

**GENDER:** Girl

**BIRTHDAY:** February 18

**BEST FEATURE:** Beautiful hair

**FAVORITE FOOD:** Cupcakes

**FAVORITE COLOR:** Pink

**HOBBIES:** Self-care, adventuring, grazing

**ATTRIBUTES:** Mysterious, sensitive, caring

# How to Tell If Your Cat Is a Unicorn

They are mysterious

They move gracefully

They are very beautiful

They are hard to find

# Pusheenicorn's Guide to Disguises

Wear a party hat

Wear a princess hat

Wear a wizard hat

Wear an ice-cream cone

# Pusheenicorn:
## The Legend

Beautiful

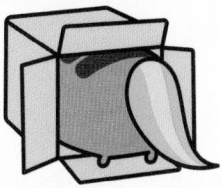

Mysterious

Magical

Sensitive

Fierce

# Essential Unicorn Skills

Galloping

Sparkling

Relaxing

Grazing

# Pusheenicorn's Motivational Tips

Accept challenges

Overcome obstacles

If things get hard . . .

you can ask for help!

# Pusheenicorn's
## BEAUTY TIPS

Admire your beauty
in a clear pool

Ponder your beauty
in a pure crystal

Gaze upon your beauty
in a silver dish

Accept your beauty
in your heart

# Pusheenicorn's Horn Tips

Use it to store snacks

Use it for ring toss

Use it for bug repellent

Use it for fashion

# Super Pusheenicorn

**GENDER:** Girl

**BIRTHDAY:** February 18

**BEST FEATURE:** Tiny but powerful wings

**FAVORITE FOOD:** Cookies

**FAVORITE COLOR:** Purple

**HOBBIES:** Flying, stargazing, self-expression

**ATTRIBUTES:** Magical, positive, energetic

# Pawsitive Affirmations with Super Pusheenicorn

Shoot for the stars

Be open to possibilities

Reach your full potential

# Happiness Essentials

## with Super Pusheenicorn

Practice acceptance

Live in the moment

Spread kindness

Be thankful

# Mermaid Pusheen

**GENDER:** Girl

**BIRTHDAY:** February 18

**BEST FEATURE:** Hair accessories

**FAVORITE FOOD:** Madeleines

**FAVORITE COLOR:** Aqua

**HOBBIES:** Swimming & watching beauty tutorials

**ATTRIBUTES:** Glamorous, fashionable, sassy

# How to Tell If Your Cat Is a Mermaid

Likes to play with water

Loves fish

Is a total diva

# Rules of the Sea

Make waves

Go with the flow

Fish are friends

Beware of sharks

# How to Get Mermaid Hair

Shampoo well

Rinse well

Apply seaweed mask

Nice work!

# Treasure Hunting 101

Go exploring

Find the spot

Start digging

Success!

# Mermaid Pusheen

Curious

Glamorous

Fashionable

Bold

# The 4 Types of Mermaid Cats

Meowmaids

Purrmaids

**Catfish**

**Bobcats**

# What's Your Swimming Style?

Backstroke

Freestyle

Butterfly

Doggy paddle

# Pusheenosaurus
## & Dinosheens

**GENDER:** Girl

**BIRTHDAY:** February 18

**BEST FEATURE:** Very tall

**FAVORITE FOOD:** Greens

**FAVORITE COLOR:** Mint

**HOBBIES:** Stomping around & swinging her tail

**ATTRIBUTES:** Strong, friendly, always hungry

# How to Tell If Your Cat Is a Dinosaur

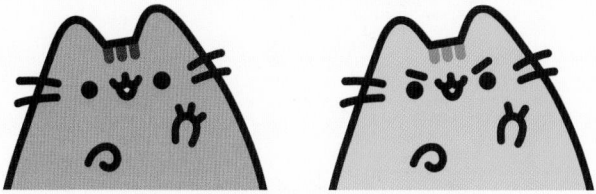

They have big claws

They have a big appetite

They're just big

# Dinosheens' Survival Guide

Run fast

Fly fast

Swim fast

Breakfast

# PUSHEENOSAURUS

Strong

Curious

Friendly

Hungry

VERY HUNGRY

Tea rex

RAWR

# How to Care for Your Pet Dinosheen

Feed them

Play with them

Brush them

Love them

Exercise them

~~Trim their nails~~

# What the T. rex May Have Looked Like

# Pastel Pusheens

**GENDER:** Girls

**BIRTHDAY:** February 18

**BEST FEATURE:** Heart-shaped markings

**FAVORITE FOOD:** Ice cream (triple scoop)

**FAVORITE COLORS:** Pink, mint, purple

**HOBBIES:** Visiting other planets & making friends

**ATTRIBUTES:** They're aliens

# How to Tell If Your Cat Is an Alien

Demands your resources

Studies your behavior

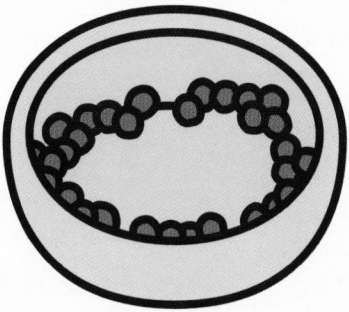

Leaves mysterious signs

Disappears at will

# "Take Us to Your Feeder"

# 6 Reasons to Consider Being an Alien

1. Travel in style

2. Broaden your horizons

3. Make new friends

4. Communicate well

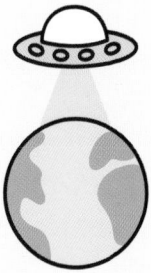

5. Invade Earth

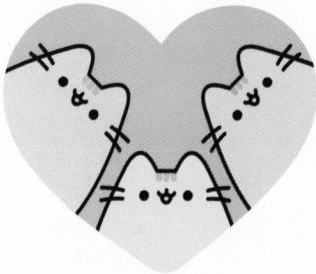

6. Invade hearts

# Pastel Pusheens' Favorite Things

Ice cream

Popsicles

Marshmallows

Each other

# Pastel Pusheens' Guide to Earthling Artifacts

"Snuggle cube"

"Food magnet"

"Fluff extractor"

"Squiggle friend"

# Anatomy of an Alien

Large eyes

Front tentacles

Teleportation mark

Back tentacle

# How to Make First Contact

Prepare a landing pad

Send out a signal

Wait for their arrival

Make a peace offering

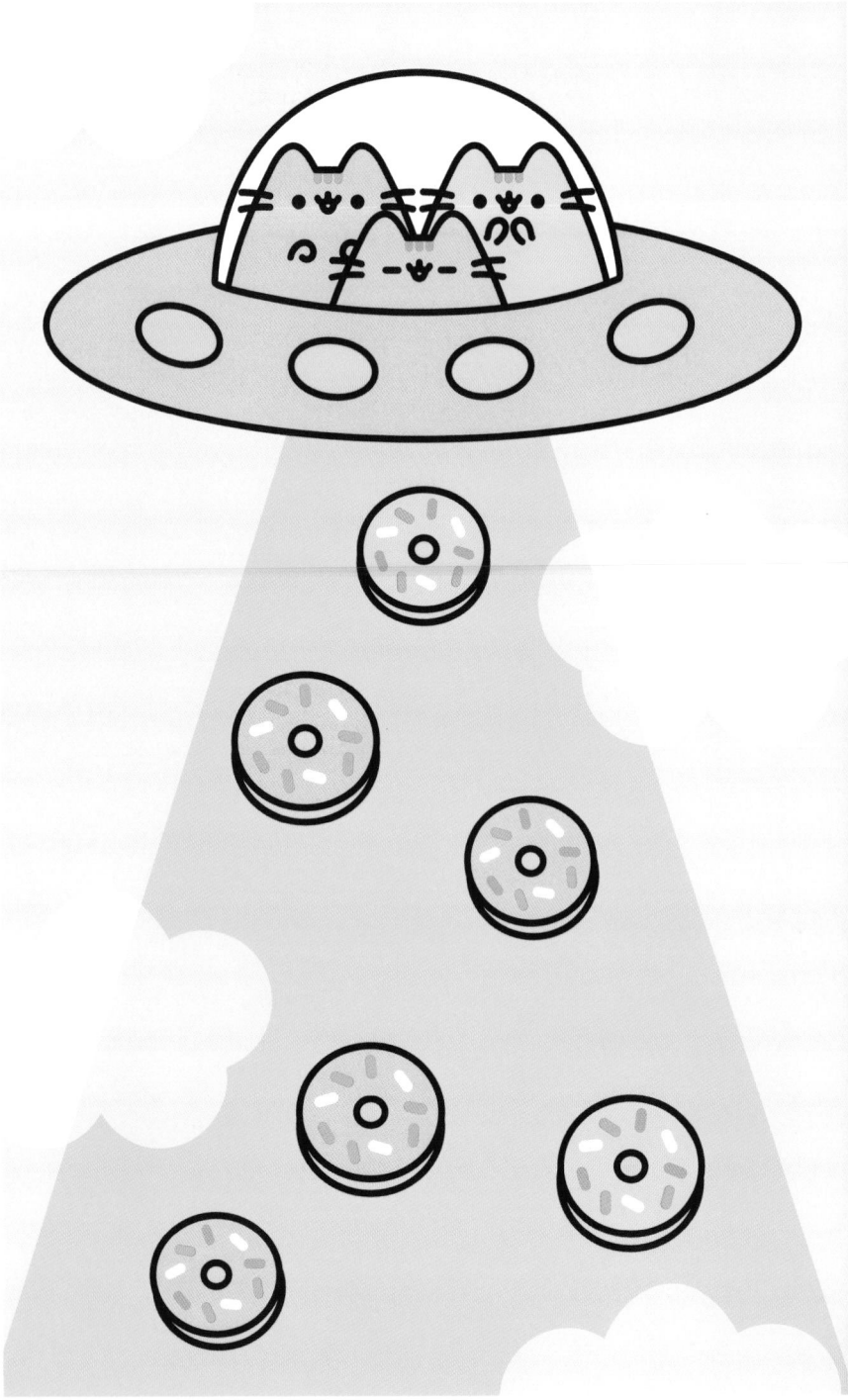

# Snacks for Aliens

UF⊙s

Star fruit

~~Human beans~~

# Pastel Pusheen

Pastel

Cute

Friendly

Uplifting

# Dragonsheen

**GENDER:** Girl

**BIRTHDAY:** February 18

**BEST FEATURE:** Dangerous breath

**FAVORITE FOOD:** Toasted marshmallows

**FAVORITE COLOR:** Gold

**HOBBIES:** Breathing fire & collecting things

**ATTRIBUTES:** Warm & cuddly

# Your Cat May Be a Dragon If . . .

They hoard treasure

They perch on high

They have dangerous breath!

# Types of Dragon Breath

Fire

Ice

Electricity

Hair

# The Life Cycle of Dragons

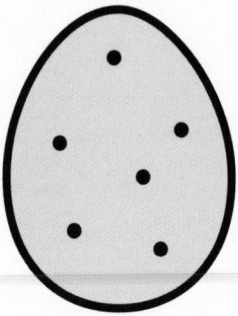

Egg

Hatchling

Young adult

Big bub

# Ways to Defend Against Dragons

Build a fort

Distract with shiny stuff

Toss a ball

Give tummy rubs

I'M BUSY

# DRAGON FRIENDS

DRAGON SLOTH

DRAGON BO

DRAGON CHEEK

DRAGON STORMY

DRAGON PIP

# Treasures Worth Keeping

Gold

Gems

Friends

Warm & cuddly

# Staying Warm with Dragonsheen

Light a cozy fire

Make fresh popcorn

Wrap up in blankets

Take a hot bath

# Dragonsheen's BBQ Techniques

Indirect cooking

Direct cooking

Smoking

Resting

# Detective Pusheen

**GENDER:** Girl

**BIRTHDAY:** February 18

**BEST FEATURE:** Her smarts

**FAVORITE FOOD:** Cookies

**FAVORITE COLOR:** Caramel

**HOBBIES:** Reading & solving mysteries

**ATTRIBUTES:** Intelligent & hardworking

# The Mystery of the Hairy Sofa

Arrive at the scene

Gather the evidence

[UNSOLVED]

# Detective Pusheen: The Mystery of the Lost Sock

Examine the scene

Review the facts

Look for clues

Tail your suspect

Case closed

# Solving the Mystery:
## Who Ate the Cookie?

# Solving the Mystery:
## A Cupboard

1. Wait for an opening

2. Enter the cupboard

3. It is dark!

4. Become frightened

5. Exit the cupboard

6. To be continued

Purrlock Holmes

# Pugsheen

**GENDER:** Girl

**BIRTHDAY:** February 18

**BEST FEATURE:** Cinnamon bun tail

**FAVORITE FOOD:** All of them

**FAVORITE COLOR:** Yellow

**HOBBIES:** Playing & going for walks

**ATTRIBUTES:** Sweet, curious, lazy

# Places That Dogs Belong

The toilet: no

Your shoes: no

The table: no

Your bag: no

This thing: ???

Your heart: yes

# How to Achieve Your Goals

Set your goal

Be flexible

Have patience

Success!

# 6 REASONS

## You Should Consider Being a Dog

1. Free food

2. Free rent

3. Sleep as long as you want to

4. Look great with no effort

5. Toes look like beans

6. Positive outlook

Naptime

# Places I Sat Yesterday

7 a.m.: a door

12 p.m.: a door

7 p.m.: a table

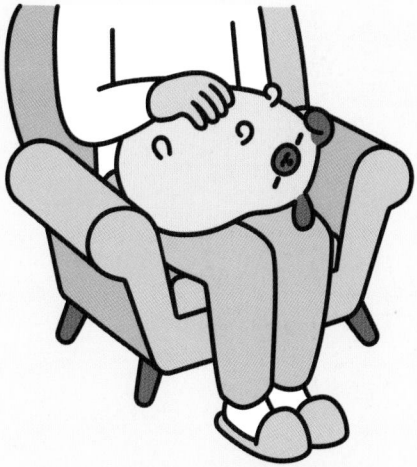

10 p.m.: a people

# Acknowledgments

I would like to sincerely thank the following people who helped make this book a reality.

First to the Pusheen creative team, whose wonderful teamwork made this endeavor (and all things Pusheen) possible:

Jess Anca
Katie Belton
Hayley Gallat
Alyson Kayne
Heather McKenna
Jing Ouyang
Kristin Ridgley
Jessica Rusher
Shane Swinnea
Jessi Zabarsky

Thanks as well to our phenomenal director of project management, Cassandra Lipin, and director of licensing, Cate D'Allessandro, whose organizational and coordination skills have been invaluable.

I would also like to thank:
My partner and Pusheen cofounder, Andrew Duff, for being my best friend and a constant source of love, support, and punny jokes.

My literary agent, Myrsini Stephanides, for all of her support, enthusiasm, and cute cat photos.

My editors at Simon & Schuster, Lauren Spiegel and Rebecca Strobel, for giving me the opportunity to publish this book, and for always supporting and believing in Pusheen.

And most importantly, to all the fans who have supported Pusheen over the last decade: Thank you so much!

# For More Pusheen, Find Her Online

www.pusheen.com

Instagram: @pusheen

Facebook: @pusheen

Twitter: @pusheen

www.youtube.com/pusheenthecat

## About the Author

Claire Belton is an artist and entrepreneur based in Chicago. She spends her time petting cats, drawing cats, and pursuing cat-related endeavors.

## About Pusheen

Pusheen is a tubby tabby cat who brings smiles and laughter to people all around the world. She became famous through her animated comics and GIFs posted on Pusheen.com, as well as through her widely used animated stickers on Facebook, Instagram, iMessage, and other platforms.

# Discover more from Pusheen!

Available wherever books are sold
or at SimonandSchuster.com

77386

GALLERY BOOKS